Wrap It Up

Wrap It Up

99 Gift-Wrapping Ideas for Birthdays, Anniversaries, and Other Occasions

Peter van der Westen
Aad de Jong

English edition and additional ideas
by Robbie Capp

Hearst Books
New York

Published in the United States of America in 1992 by William Morrow and
Company, 1350 Avenue of the Americas, New York, N.Y. 10019

First published in The Netherlands in 1992 by Unieboek b.v., PO Box 97,
3990 DB Houten, The Netherlands

ISBN 0-688-11208-0 LC 91-36040

Printed in Hong Kong

First Edition

1 2 3 4 5 6 7 8 9 10

BOOK DESIGN BY JACK BOTERMANS

CONTENTS

INTRODUCTION

Part of the fun of receiving a gift is the way it's presented. Even the simplest offering takes on a special excitement when it's wrapped with care and flair. This book will tell you how.

Following clear, step-by-step instructions utilizing papers, ribbons, and other packing materials that are widely available (see page 64 for a guide to gift-wrapping materials and tools), you'll learn basic gift-wrapping techniques to embellish every birthday, anniversary, holiday, and special-occasion gift on your list.

Instructions include making your own unusually shaped gift boxes. It's not only more creative to construct your own, but more economical than buying ready-made ones. For prepackaged items, with the wealth of beautifully patterned wrapping papers on the market, plus ribbons, cords, and yarns in a myriad of colors – and lots of inventive ideas in these pages for putting them all together – you can design gift wraps tailored to the occasion, the personality, and the taste of each recipient.

The old saying "It's the thought that counts" is particularly appropriate here. A little thought, time, and ingenuity can dress up a gift far beyond its intrinsic value, and provide a pleasurable shared event for giver and receiver alike.

GIFT WRAP WITH A PERSONAL TOUCH

When you buy a prepackaged item or one that fits into a standard box, many stores will furnish the box and gift wrap it for you. But it's so much more personal to do the outer wrap yourself. You can customize your selection of paper, ribbon, and trim to the person's age group, particular style, or the occasion that prompts the gift.

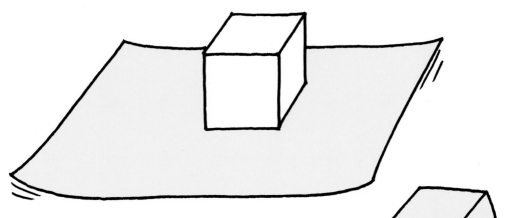

Basics: How to Wrap a Box

Many people have problems wrapping a box, simply because they begin with the wrong size sheet of paper. While the exact dimensions depend on the size of the box to be wrapped, a good general rule is: Cut your paper wide enough to wrap completely around the package, plus a bit extra for overlap, and long enough to fold fully over the ends. If the sheet is too long, it's hard to fold the ends neatly; if it's too short, it won't cover the box ends completely.

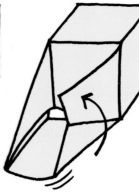
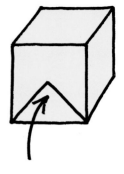

A. Center the box on the paper as shown.

B. Roll the paper lengthwise creasing the edges sharply as you go. The ends should overlap slightly (the overlap can be folded under or left flat). Secure the paper with transparent tape. There are three ways to fold the ends. In the method illustrated here:

C. Fold the paper downward and crease sharply.

D. Then fold inward and crease.

E. The triangular flap that results is then folded upward and taped closed. A second method – good for larger packages – is to fold the two shorter sides inward and crease. This forms triangular flaps at the top and bottom, which are then folded over, creased, and taped. The third way is best for flatter packages (books, records, compact discs). First fold the top and sides inward;

then fold the bottom once or twice, each fold being equal to the thickness of the package so that the join lies along one edge.

F. For a classic gift wrap, finish the package off with a ribbon circling all sides, ending with a simple bow centered on top.

Tips

1. Instead of ribbon, as a variation seal your package with colored tape or thick yarn.
2. Design your own sheet of wrapping paper: Cut oblongs from a few papers of different patterns and glue or tape them together.

BOWS, ROSETTES, AND OTHER BASIC RIBBON TRIM

When you go to the gift-wrap counter in a fine department store and watch the pro dress your package, don't you wish you could make that big beautiful bow the way she did? You can, if you study the illustrations and step-by-step instructions that follow for making basic bows and several varieties of ribbon trim to top your gift. The simpler forms will look more luxe if you use wider ribbon (1 inch – 2.5 cm – or more), but it's easier to make more complex bows and decorations with narrower ribbon (3/4 inches – 2 cm – or less). Choose a color to match, highlight, or complement your wrapping-paper color.

The Basic Decorative Bow
A. The easiest way to make a simple bow is to place a length of ribbon in a circle and join the ends with a spot of glue or a bit of transparent adhesive tape. Cut a narrower strip of matching ribbon. Now close your circle of ribbon where you glued it by pressing that point against the opposite side of the circumference, making a figure-eight loop. Secure it with your short piece of matching ribbon in an overhand knot. Note: The length of ribbon you start with and the width of your finished bow are roughly a three-to-one ratio. For example, if you want a bow that's 6 inches wide (about 15 cm) loop end to loop end, start with an 18-inch (45 cm) length of ribbon.

11

B. For a double bow, make two separate bows, then place them either back to back or at angles to each other and tie off with narrower ribbon as above.

The Rosette or Multiple Bow

C. First make a number of bows from separate lengths of ribbons, as described above. Start with three or four and build up to five or six after you've practiced a bit. Arrange the bows attractively and tie them together as above. If you're not satisfied with the look of your bow cluster, fan out the loops for better balance. For variety, you can also cut through some loops and give those ends a diagonal, pointed, or V-shaped cut.

D. Ridged curling ribbon, drawn across the end of a scissors blade, produces pretty spiral ends.

E. After you've become experienced at making bows, experiment by building multiple loops made from ribbon of different widths. Try for an unusual look by using differing lengths of ribbon to tie the loops together.

Tips

1. For a bright variation, combine two different ribbon colors for your multiple-bow rosette.

2. When you use wide ribbon, you may find it easier to tie the loops together if you cut V-shaped notches at the point where the loops are to be tied.

3. Experiment by combining all of the above techniques: Create your own original by mixing wide and narrow ribbons, ribbons in two different colors, and some cut-through loops with shaped ends – all in one large, lavish bow.

The One-Piece Rosette

A. Place your ribbon in a circle and tape the ends together. The length of ribbon depends on its width and the size rosette you'd like. For example: If you use 3/4-inch (2 cm) ribbon, cut a 48-inch (120 cm) length, which will produce a rosette with a diameter of about 4 inches (10 cm). Roll up the ribbon – one complete roll for each double loop. Tape the end in place.

B. Now form your double loops by pressing the rolled-up circle closed from opposite sides of its circumference. Cut little V notches at this center point. Using a thin strip of the same ribbon, tie across the V notches. Remove the tape that held the loops.

C. Starting at the center, tease the loops apart between thumb and fingers, working from left to right, opening them out until you get a fully balanced rosette. Use the tails of the join strip to attach to the ribbon that goes around your box, or if using the rosette alone, tuck the tails under and tape to your package.

The Bow Tie

Simple as A, B, C, the bow tie is made from three pieces of ribbon.

A. Make a flat bow out of a long strip.

B. Tape a short strip around it.

C. Tape the flat bow to a third strip of ribbon and affix it to your package with two-sided adhesive tape. For a bright variation, use three different colors for your A, B, C ribbon strips.

The Spiral

Stiff paper ribbon (or a strip cut from wrapping paper) works best for this contemporary trim.

A. For the five-loop spiral shown, using 3/4-inch ribbon (2 cm), cut a piece about 26 inches (65 cm) long. Start with a small loop and tape it, then make four more loops, each progressively larger. Secure the final loop on the underside with tape, then add two-sided tape to fasten it to your package. For a variation:

B. Press the spiral flat under a heavy book for a few minutes. The crease will give your spiral a leafy look.

The Spiral Accordion

C. For a handsome tailored variation, give your spiral an accordion-pleated base. Cut a long, wide strip of paper (same paper used for spiral), pleat it, tape spiral to the center, fan the pleats open, and attach with two-sided tape to your package.

CROSS AT THE CORNER

Here's a terrific example of how ingenuity can turn a usual gift wrap into an unusual one. While you may not find the particular paper shown in this photo, the wrapping idea would adapt nicely to any paper that has a bold geometric design. In this case, a pink zig-zag pattern on a peacock-blue ground is combined with a ribbon that picks up the pink in the paper. Also note that the angle the ribbon follows as it crosses the box corners parallels the angle of the zigzag pattern, creating a smart, coordinated look. To get this effect, be sure your paper and ribbon colors are well matched.

and sides of the package, and the broken lines show the path of the ribbon underneath. Start your ribbon at the lower left arrow, pull it under the box to the upper right corner, then lead it over and under the package as illustrated. (You might find it helps to use a spot of two-sided tape underneath to keep the ribbon from slipping off the corners.) After the final corner turn, the two ends can be tied off in a bow. Then curl the trailing ends slightly for a final flourish.

Tips

1. Use different ribbon colors for opposite ends of the package, by starting with two different colors of equal length taped together.
2. For a reverse variation, use solid–color paper and patterned ribbon–checkered is a good choice.

How to Cross the Corner
This ribbon decoration works best on fairly flat, prepackaged items such as board games or stationery. A. First wrap and seal your package in the conventional way. Now note in the sketch that the unbroken lines show how the ribbon goes across the top

LOVE(LY) TRIANGLE

An expensive gift for someone you love deserves a presentation that announces something special is inside. How about an unusual box shape? One that's seldom used in commercial packaging is a triangle. Of course, you'll have to make your own, which further emphasizes the specialness of the gift. Save this sophisticated package for smaller, luxurious gifts such as jewelry for a woman, a gold money clip for a man, or a glass paperweight or other small objet d'art as a house gift. Instructions follow for making the box. Then choose an elegant metallic paper for your outer wrap, and top it off with a rosette or flat bow in matching or contrasting color.

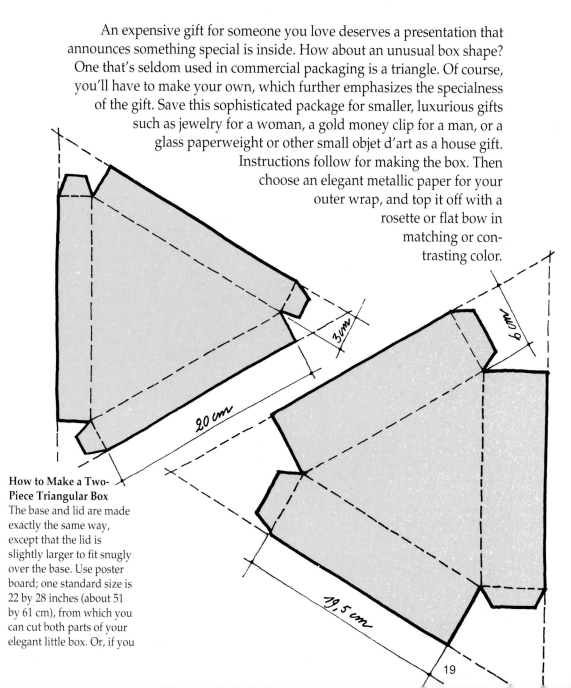

How to Make a Two-Piece Triangular Box
The base and lid are made exactly the same way, except that the lid is slightly larger to fit snugly over the base. Use poster board; one standard size is 22 by 28 inches (about 51 by 61 cm), from which you can cut both parts of your elegant little box. Or, if you

19

prefer, use contrasting colors for base and lid. As for size: For jewelry or a money clip, a triangle with 4-inch (10 cm) sides would be about right; for a paperweight, 8-inch (20 cm) sides should do.

Start by turning your poster board over. Using pencil and ruler (steel is best), for an 8-inch triangle draw an 8-inch (20 cm) horizontal base line. To get the other two sides of your equilateral triangle, first rule a light vertical line up from the center of your base line, at right angles to it. Then slant your ruler and draw an 8-inch (20 cm) line from the left end of your base line to the center vertical line. Rule your final 8-inch line from the right end of the base line up to the center, and your triangle is completed.

Now, referring to the illustrations:

A. Starting with the box lid, your triangle represents the inside broken line in the illustration. Using the marked measurements as a guide, rule in the sides of the lid, with their flaps, as shown in the sketch.

B. Now rule the base of your box, drawing in the side flaps as you did for the lid. But note the difference: The base is slightly smaller than the lid (7-5/8-inch base for an 8-inch lid) but twice as deep (9-3/8-inch base takes an 1-3/16-inch lid). After base and lid are fully drawn, carefully cut out both complete shapes, using a hobby knife or sharp scissors. Now referring to the broken lines in both sketches (the center triangles), score along those lines, and the flap lines. If you use a hobby knife for scoring, be careful not to cut through the cardboard. Safer tools are a blunt butter knife or the end of a large paper clip, pressed against a steel ruler held along the line to be scored.

C. Bend the board inward along the scored lines and crease sharply. Next, assemble the base and lid in the same way – by pasting each flap to its adjacent side. Hold the joins firmly in place with clothespins or big paper clips to give the glue a chance to set. After you've placed your gift inside the box, put the lid on and you're ready for the outer wrap.

D. Your sheet of paper should be square and just a

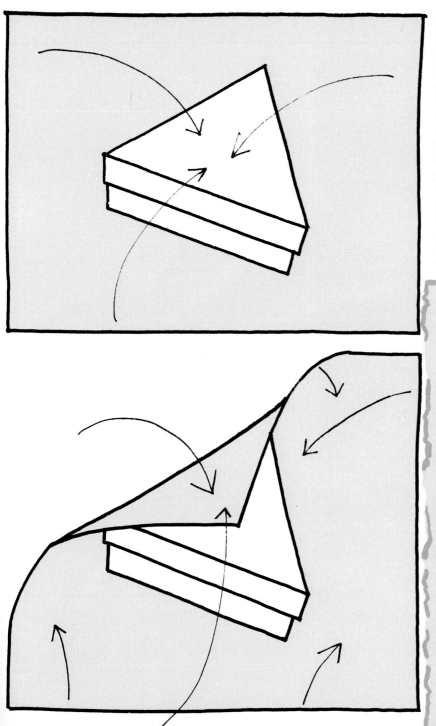

bit larger than the box length, as illustrated. (If the sheet is too large, you'll have trouble folding and creasing the corners.)

E. Wrap the box in the usual way, starting at one corner and working clockwise, folding in and creasing the corners as you go, then finishing them off with a small piece of transparent tape. A nice detail for the final adornment would be a simple bow tie for a man's gift, a full rosette for a woman's.

Tips

1. Poster board (or oaktag) is available in lots of colors. If you use two different colors for base and lid, you may prefer to leave the box unwrapped. This is especially effective when the base is twice as deep as the lid, since both colors are fully visible.

2. Boxes with five, six, or eight sides can be made in nearly the same way. The basic shapes can be drawn with compasses and a protractor, to measure the angles, but if mechanical drawing isn't for you, plastic templates can be found in art-supply stores.

THE FAN TRIM

Here's one of the most charming of all package adornments – especially when combined with a big rosette bow – yet it's also one of the simplest to make. The fan trim will enhance any gift, but it's most compatible with flat, oblong boxes, (neckties, gloves) or square packages (belts, scarves).

How to Make the Fan

After you've wrapped your box, take another piece of the same wrapping paper, sized according to how full a fan you want: The more pleats, the longer the paper.

A. Lay the sheet of paper on a flat surface. Fold one edge over and crease sharply. With the width of your first fold as your guide, fold again and crease, and again, progressively across the whole sheet.

B. Curl a long strip of narrow ribbon and tie it around your closed fan about one-quarter the way in from one end.

C. Now open out the fan. Attach it with glue or two-sided tape to your package.

D. Round out the decoration by adding a big rosette to the base of the fan.

Tips

1. For a multicolored fan, piece strips of differentpapers together with transparent tape, and fold in the same way as above. (Each strip should make three or four folds.)

2. Use a floral paper for the fan, and a solid paper for the box wrap, choosing a color dominant in the floral pattern.

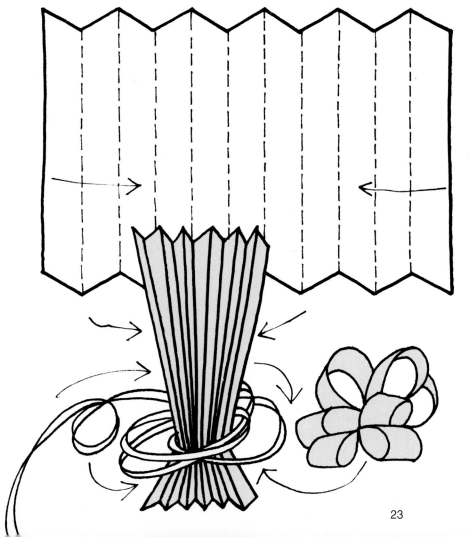

ABOUT ROUND PACKAGES

Many popular and functional gifts are prepackaged in cylindrical containers: canisters of tennis balls; posters in long tubes; rolls of wrapping paper (a thoughtful gift!); and some colognes and dusting powders. The instructions that follow can be adapted to almost any contoured container – even shallow tins of cookies or candy.

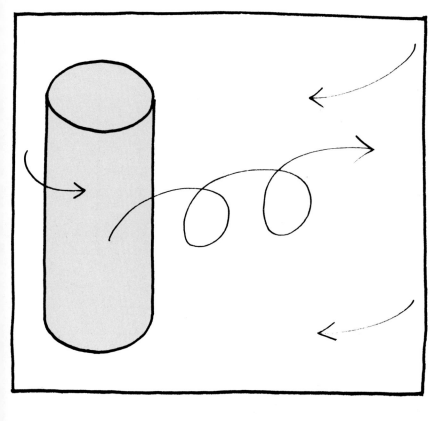

How to Wrap Cylindrical Containers

Choose a sheet of paper wide enough to go around your cylinder (twice around if the paper is thin), plus some extra for overlap. The sheet should be long enough to cover both ends.

A. Lay the cylinder at one end of the sheet, as shown.

B. The overlap can be sealed neatly with a length of transparent or colored tape.

C. Fold the paper at one end and tape; do the same thing at the other end.

D. Decorate your cylinder with narrow lengths of ribbon or thick yarn. The package in the photo on page 25 was made with two lengths of light-blue ribbon and two of pink; the page 27 example uses only two lengths.

E. To assemble, hold one length of ribbon at the top of the package, lead it

Tips

1. Papers of subtle pastel tones or traditional floral patterns look especially well on round containers. Wallpaper with classic Victorian designs is ideal, and has nice heavy weight, too. Select thick yarn or narrow ribbon in colors that complement your paper.

2. If you use solid-color paper, dress up your package with decals.

3. Save jars and round tins for wrapping a wide variety of gifts; all kinds of homemade food goodies; jigsaw puzzle pieces; a big bunch of colored pencils; or small clothing items, such as socks or belts.

down the side, under the base, and back up to the top. Knot it tightly. Attach the other ribbons in the same way. The knots are concealed by the ribbon rosette mounted on top of the package. (See page 12–14, for rosette instructions.) For the prettiest effect, make the rosette about the same width as the package.

ENVELOPE IT

This envelope box, made of shimmering cardboard, is handsome enough to serve as a permanent home for the gift it encloses – perhaps leather gloves, a compact camera, or decks of playing cards, as shown here. Note the regal color combination – gold box with narrow gold and wide blue ribbon.

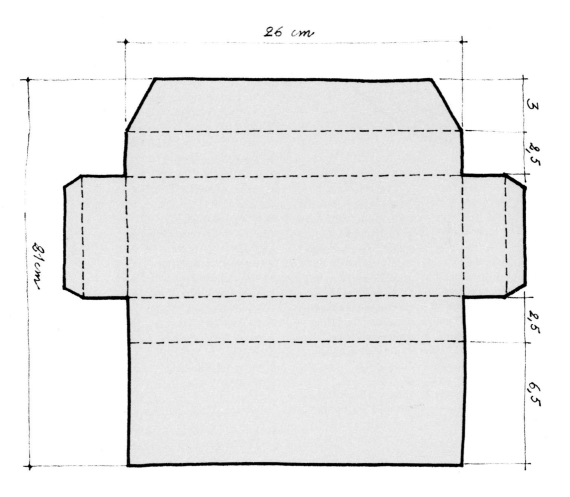

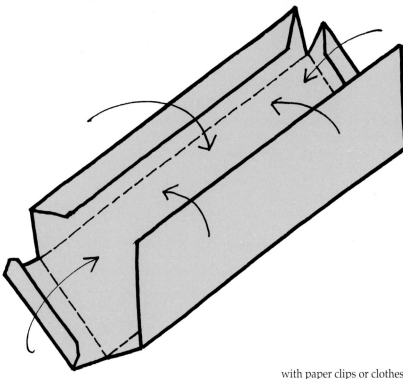

How to Make the Envelope Box

Measure your gift item to determine how large your box must be. The dimensions given here are for two decks of playing cards.

A. With pencil and ruler, draw the opened-out envelope shape on the back of a sheet of poster board. Drafting tools such as a T-square and triangle are useful, but you can also use a book edge to get your right angles squared off. Carefully cut out the entire shape with a hobby knife or sharp scissors. Angle the corners of the top flap as shown. Score along the broken lines with hobby knife and ruler (steel is best), being careful not to cut through the cardboard – or use a blunt butter knife or end of a large paper clip for scoring.

B. Bend the cardboard inward along the scored lines and crease firmly. Fold in sides and side flaps. Fold the front over and glue it to the flaps. Hold these joins in place with paper clips or clothespins until the glue sets.

C. Insert your gift and fold the lid down.

D. Wrap ribbon around your envelope box to keep the lid closed. Finish it off with a bow and notch the ends. The final trim is thin gold curling ribbon on the blue satin ribbon (conceal the knot under the ribbon bow), its trailing ends drawn across a scissors blade to create pretty spirals.

Tips

1. If you can't find gold poster board, use plain cardboard and cover it with gold foil wrapping paper. Cardboard covered with aluminum foil will produce a glimmery silver finish.

2. Instead of a single bow, you might use a large rosette, but eliminate the gold ribbon.

THE SEEMINGLY SEAMLESS WRAP

There are several ways to wrap a package so that the overlaps and joins of the paper won't show. Here's one of the neatest methods, but it does require careful measuring and cutting to make it work perfectly. It's an ideal wrap for an ever-growing category of gifts – compact discs, cassettes, and videos – since fairly flat, prepackaged items are good candidates for this clean, tailored, seamless look.

How to Conceal Paper Seams

The trick to this gift wrap is that the final flap folds over to conceal the other overlaps and joins.

A. Referring to the sketch: The broken-line square in the center represents the item to be wrapped. The broken lines at the four corners show where the paper has been cut away to produce the four flaps. Following the arrows, first fold the top flap down and the bottom flap up; tape in place.

B. Next fold the flap on the right over to the left, and tape. The final fold is the left flap which, as you can see, is the largest, to cover the width of the package plus its thickness. It should fold over to reach the right edge exactly, where it is sealed with double-sided transparent tape. Add ribbon trim, plus a rosette (pages 11-15).

Tips

1. If your gift is a compact disc, simulate its look as a decoration for the box. Take aluminum foil, cut out a circle the size of the CD, cut a hole in its center, and glue it to your outer wrap, for a bright, bull's-eye effect.

2. Another neat tailored look, especially for a man's gift, is random placement of simple geometric shapes – squares, circles, triangles – cut from ordinary white self-stick mailing labels to adorn a navy-blue or forest-green glossy wrap.

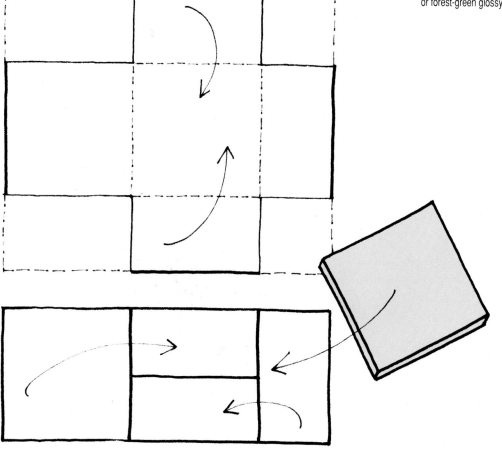

33

TRIPLE-TREAT TRIM

Any box can be made a standout with this easy yet distinctive three-ribbon decoration. For best effect, coordinate ribbon and paper colors. In the package shown, the green, yellow, and silver-gray in the paper are repeated in the ribbon colors. A multicolored striped paper tied with a trio of its tones would also be a good choice.

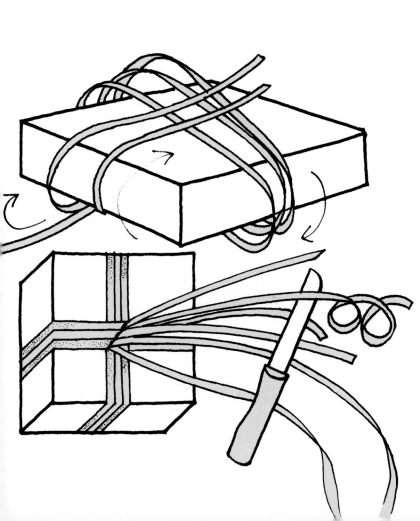

How to Make Three-Ribbon Trim

Select a patterned paper and pick out three of its colors to replicate in ribbon colors. Wrap your box in the usual way. Decide the best arrangement of your three ribbon colors, then:

A. Wrap the first length of ribbon around the center of the box, cross it over itself and bring it around again at right angles to the first direction. When you get back to where you started, knot the ribbon firmly in place, leaving two long ends. Repeat this procedure with the other two ribbons, checking to see that they're straight and abut neatly; and align the three knots.

B. Leave one end of each ribbon straight, and curl the other end – for a lively mix of three streamers and three curlicues.

Tip

Instead of always using bright colors, conservative neutrals can make stylish packages, too. Start with a chocolate-brown glossy wrapping paper and use beige, rust, and cream-colored ribbons.

HEARTFELT GIFT:
THE VALENTINE ACCORDION

This original, easily assembled package owes its stunning looks to the great care that went into selecting paper and package accessories. The beautifully patterned paper, lush rosette bow, and velvet hearts are in subtle variations of rich red. Even the gift card, also in deep red, was thoughtfully chosen to heighten the holiday flavor. This package was designed to give to a lover on Valentine's Day, or a spouse or Significant Other to mark an anniversary. But you might also consider it for a wedding-gift wrap – an unexpected variation on all the white-and-silver wraps brides and grooms usually receive.

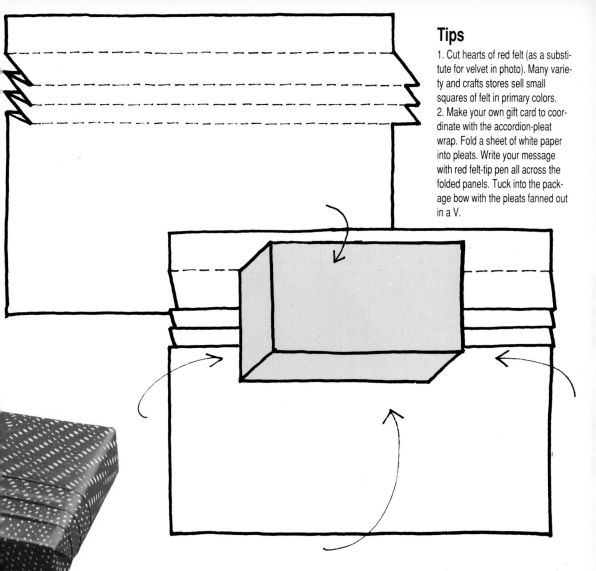

Tips

1. Cut hearts of red felt (as a substitute for velvet in photo). Many variety and crafts stores sell small squares of felt in primary colors.
2. Make your own gift card to coordinate with the accordion-pleat wrap. Fold a sheet of white paper into pleats. Write your message with red felt-tip pen all across the folded panels. Tuck into the package bow with the pleats fanned out in a V.

How to Make the Valentine Accordion Wrap

A. After choosing your materials with care, cut your paper sheet to the appropriate size, flatten it out, and make three accordion pleats, as shown. So that the folds will remain sharp, put a big book or other heavy object on top of them for about an hour. B. Place your gift box on the folds in the position shown, then wrap in the conventional manner. First fold over the sides, then the ends, and secure with transparent tape.

Wrap a length of ribbon around the package, fairly near one end, to hold the rosette. Make your rosette (see pages 12-14), and mount it on the ribbon with a spot of glue or a well-concealed paper clip. Pin on two heart decorations and place the card – with its appropriate message of undying love – into the rose.

CHEERFUL WRAP FOR A BOTTLE OF CHEER

What could be a more welcome gift than a bottle of vintage wine?
Not only suitable as birthday, anniversary, or holiday gifts, wine,
spirits, and liqueurs are gracious traditional thank-you offerings to
the host of a dinner party or other event. Have the gift please the
eye as well as the palate by wrapping the bottle festively.

How to Wrap a Bottle
Since the top of this wrap lets you see the inside of the paper, an ideal choice would be one whose pattern shows on both sides – or has a design on one side and a silver lining on the other. Or, you can easily make your silver lining by pasting aluminum foil on the back of any pretty solid or patterned paper you choose.

The sheet should be wide enough to wrap completely around the bottle, plus some overlap, and it should be about one-and-a-half times as long as the bottle.

A. Spread the sheet out with foil side up and place the bottle at one end, a couple of inches from the bottom of the sheet. Roll it up in the conventional way, securing the overlap with transparent tape. Fold the paper over the bottom of the bottle and tape lightly.

B. Twist the paper around the bottle neck and tie it up using ribbon that's color-coordinated to the paper. A final flourish is added with narrow curling ribbon, color matched to the first ribbon, its ends drawn across a scissors blade to make long spirals.

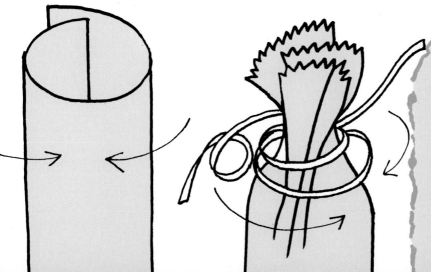

Tips
1. Coordinate the dominant color of the paper to the contents of the bottle: Red for wine or port; white or silvery-gray for vodka, gin; green for crème de menthe, and so on.
2. For a sharp look, cut zigzags around the top edge of the paper, and spread it open a bit so that the foil lining shows. If you have pinking shears, use it to make a neat, saw-toothed edge.

39

THE LOVE-ME-KNOT PACKAGE

An old Japanese custom inspired this package design. Legend has it that hundreds of years ago sweethearts folded their love letters in the form of a simple overhand knot. This adaptation of the lover's knot is suitable only for small, foldable gifts such as neckties, knee socks, leotards, or tights.

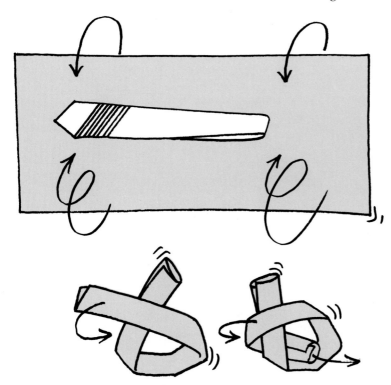

Position your gift item lengthwise, as illustrated. Now roll it up to form a long, flat package.

B. At about a fourth of the way in from the left, fold the end up at a 45-degree-angle, as shown.

C. Do the same thing on the right end of the package, crossing it over in front of the left.

D. Pass the right side under and pull it through. If necessary, adjust the shape and position of the knot, then smooth it out flat. The most important thing is to get the three different paper colors into the positions shown in the photo. This may be hard to do at first, but, as they say, practice (and patience) makes perfect.

How to Tie the Lover's Knot

Start with three sheets of tissue paper in three different colors, each sheet doubled.

A. Overlap and stagger the sheets lengthwise and widthwise, so that all three colors show.

Tips

1. First make the lover's knot from a single sheet of paper. When you've mastered the technique, try it with three sheets. You'll find it easier to do it you glue or tape the sheets together at their overlaps.

2. Gifts such as handkerchiefs can be folded and knotted in this way themselves, without an outer wrap. The initials of the gift recipient can then be stenciled or stitched on the knot.

THE CATERPILLAR WRAP

The usual way to wrap several similar objects is to assemble them all in a box. A more clever way is to line them up and enclose them in this cute caterpillar wrap, ideal for small round or oval objects such as golf or Ping-Pong balls, Easter eggs, or spherical candles. With larger numbers of small items – hard candies, Christmas-tree ornaments – a really long caterpillar can be lots of fun to make and receive. The caterpillar is also a delightful wrap for fresh or dried fruits taken to a hospital patient.

How to Make the Caterpillar Wrap

All you need are two sheets of suitably sized tissue or crepe paper laid one on top of the other, the same or different colors. The package has added charm when the ends are zigzagged, which can be cut with ordinary scissors but is easier and more uniform when done with pinking shears (dressmakers' sawtoothed scissors).

A. Line the objects up along the center of the paper with some gap between them and about 2 inches (5 cm) at each end. Roll the paper carefully, and tie off both ends with standard bows of narrow ribbon, thick yarn, or metallic cord.

B. Make a full twist in the paper between objects and tie each twist with a simple bow.

Tips

1. Instead of tissue paper, polka-dot wrapping paper would be nicely compatible with the rounded contours of the package.

2. Use remnants of knitting yarn in different colors for each tie.

3. Gifts of dried fruits should be wrapped in aluminum or wax paper first, before applying the outer wrap.

ANOTHER TRIANGLE

Here's another version of the triangular package shown on page 19. It's included again to emphasize the versatility of this box design, and the flexibility of its size. Made in two pieces, the size and depth of the triangle can be adapted to the item it's to contain: A large, deep box for a lacy nightgown – small and shallow for a pair of earrings. In the photo shown here, the package is adorned by a beautiful three-dimensional silver star and curled ribbon. Such rich embellishment signals a luxurious gift inside: perhaps a silk handkerchief folded into a triangle for the breast pocket of a man's suit.

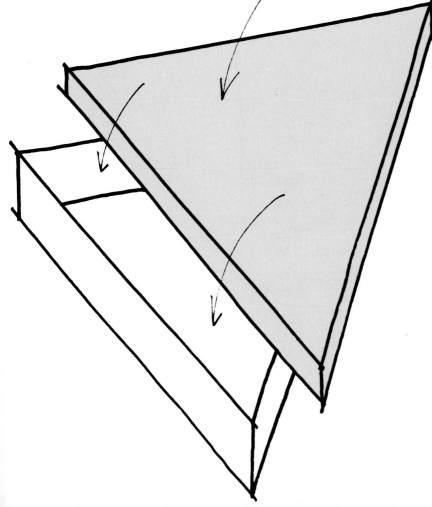

How to Make the Two-Piece Triangular Box

The base and lid are made in the same way, the only difference being their dimensions.

A. The base is twice as deep as the lid, but the sides of the lid are a bit longer to fit snugly over the base. Obviously, the measurements in the following illustrations can be sized up or down for larger or smaller gifts. For a two-toned box, start with two contrasting sheets of colored cardboard – blue and gray make a chic combination.

B. Rule your box base on the back of the cardboard. Using pencil and ruler (steel is best), draw one side (approximately 8 inches long) of the triangle first, find its center, and rule a vertical line up from it at right angles. Now slant your ruler, and from

19,5 cm

6 cm

the left end of your first line, draw another 8-inch line over to the vertical line. Rule your final 8-inch line from the right end of the base line up to the center line, and your triangle is completed.

C. Repeat the procedure for the lid, adjusting the measurements accordingly. On both drawings, add lines (follow broken lines in illustrations) where the base and lid sides are to be scored. Place a ruler on the line, and run a butter knife or one end of a large paper clip against it to score.

D. Fold in and crease firmly along score lines, fold in the flaps, and glue in place. Clothespins or paper clips can hold the joins until the glue sets.

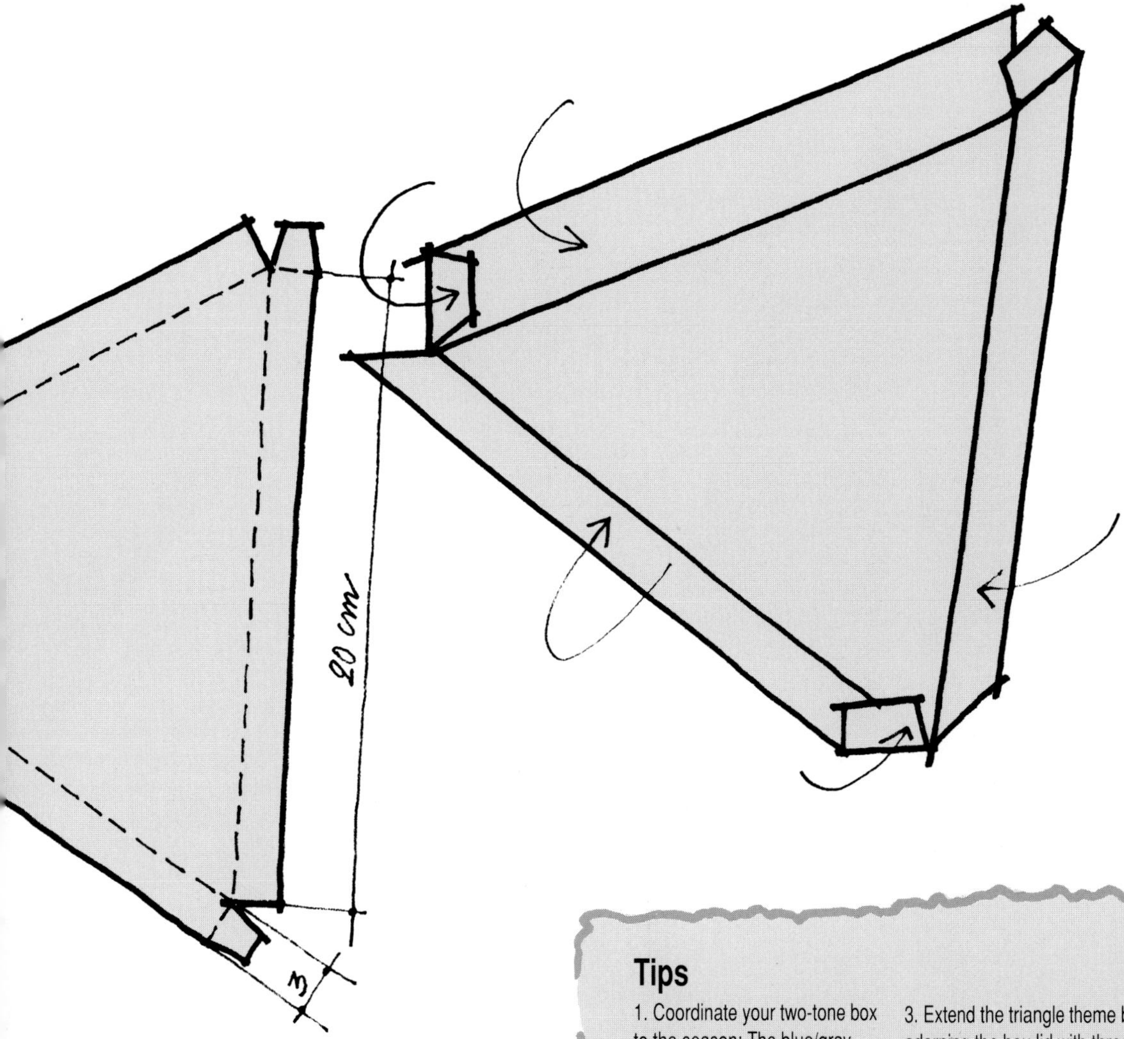

20 cm

3

Tips

1. Coordinate your two-tone box to the season: The blue/gray pairing for winter; yellow/orange for summer; green/pink for spring; rust/brown for fall.
2. When giving jewelry, line your box with cotton or tissue.

3. Extend the triangle theme by adorning the box lid with three small triangles cut from silver or gold foil and glued to the corners of your box lid.

THE COOKIE-TIN WRAP

One of the more usual items packaged in round, shallow tins gives this gift wrap its name. In addition to cookies, other food items, such as candies, cheeses and crackers that come in tins can be dressed up like this.

How to Make the Cookie-Tin Wrap

A square sheet of fairly heavy but pliable paper is best for this package. Soft, thick tissue with a marbleized design can sometimes be found in specialty craft stores, but if not available where you shop, use standard tissue, doubled. The sheet should be about three times the diameter of the gift you're going to wrap. It's a simple two-step procedure: A. Place the container in the center of the paper, bring the four corners up and bunch the paper to form a neck. B. Tie a broad ribbon with an attractive bow around the neck. Embellish with sprays of dried leaves, ferns, or flowers. (A second, narrower ribbon or cord can be added around the neck to hold the florals in place.)

Tips

1. You can make your own arrangements of dried leaves or ferns quite easily. Clusters of leaves in rich shades of brown, russet, and yellow can be found in fall. Treat these with a transparent varnish fixative, or spray them with gold or silver paint. Ferns can be pressed (or dried slowly in a cooling oven) and then treated in a similar way.
2. Line your cookie tin in aluminum foil and before closing the lid, bring the foil over the side of the tin and scallop or zigzag the edges.

THE DOUBLE-DIAGONAL WRAP

Here's a good example of how to transform an ordinary package into an extraordinary one. Three different papers are joined, and the whole sheet is folded twice diagonally. Then the box is placed on the diagonal and wrapped. As the photo shows, it's puzzling to see just how this intriguing double diagonal was achieved. Save this idea for oblong items that are not too thick: books, picture frames, boxed shirts, pajamas.

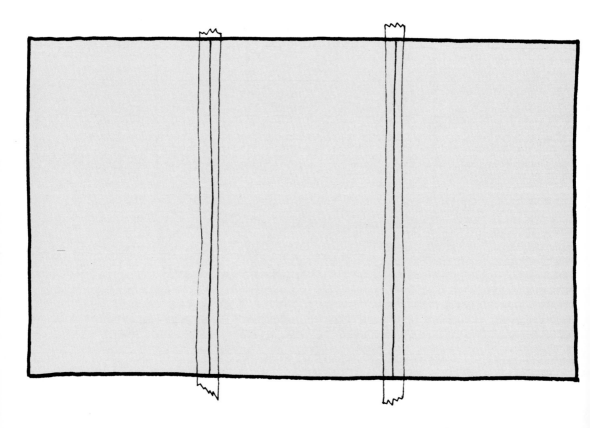

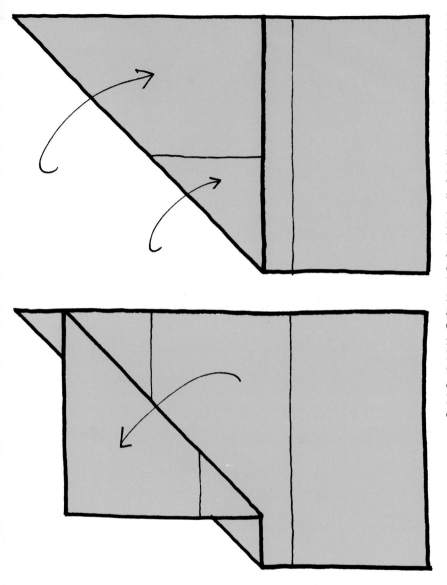

How to Make the Double-Diagonal Wrap

First select three different papers in colors and/or patterns that work well together. You'll get a lovely effect by combining two solid colors with a patterned paper. Check the size of the item to be wrapped, and cut three lengths of paper of appropriate size.

A. Working on a flat surface, place the sheets side by side – pattern side up – and join the seams with clear or colored tape.

B. Make a deep fold up from the bottom left corner and crease sharply.

C. Turn this fold back over itself and crease.

D. Flip the paper over so that the patterned side is downward.

E. Place your gift in the diagonal position shown.

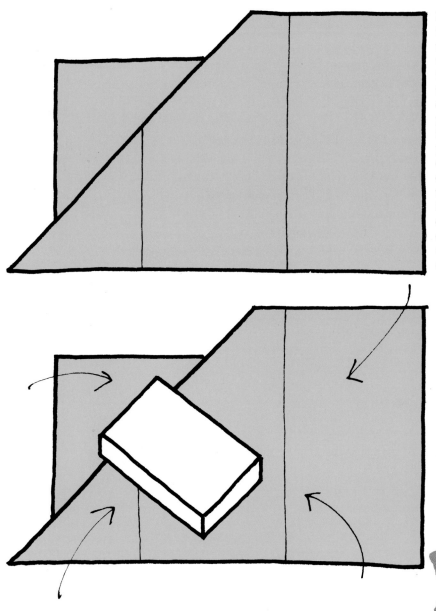

Following the arrows on the illustration, start at the upper left corner and fold the paper down, wrapping the paper in the conventional fashion, working clockwise. If you have a problem folding and creasing the corners, perhaps you need to trim off some excess paper. You might embellish your finished wrap with a spray of dried flowers or ferns – but take care that it's incidental enough not to detract from the striking effect of the diagonal folds.

Tips

1. If you have a larger gift to wrap, see what a great look you'll get by using four different papers, – two solids, two patterned – placed alternately.
2. Mix three totally different and clashing patterns for a really wild,

THE THREE-PIECE CYLINDRICAL WRAP

Many welcome gifts come in bottles - not only wine, but fancy foods such as imported vinegar and olive oil, and some unboxed large-size colognes, after-shave, or bubble bath. Here's a variation on the earlier bottle wrap (page 39). It's also a way to wrap things that come rolled up in tubes (posters, maps), or need the protection of one (glass items especially). You can easily make an open-ended cylinder by simply rolling up a sheet of cardboard and taping the seam. It's a useful container for a wide variety of gifts ranging from dolls to flower vases to stemware.

How to Make the Three-Piece Cylindrical Wrap Mix and match three papers of different colors or patterns that blend well together. Measure the length of the bottle or cylinder to be wrapped. From each of two of your sheets of paper cut a rectangular piece a little longer than the bottle or cylin- der. From the third sheet of paper cut a rectangular piece equal to the combined widths of the first two sheets.

A. Position the three sheets as shown, face up, and join the seams with gold or silver adhesive tape. Turn your assembled sheet over so that the tape faces down. Lay the bottle or cylinder across one corner diagonally, and roll it up to the other corner, attaching the overlap point with tape. Fold the paper at the base and tape in place.

B. Fold the top ends down as illustrated, and secure with a staple. Crown your gift with a single or small rosette bow attached to the flap.

Tips

1. Use a striped paper, but cut your three sections of paper on different angles for an abstract geometric pattern.

2. Mix papers of the same color but different textures; glossy, a matte finish, and crepe paper.

THE ROSE PACKAGE

Traditionally, a long-stemmed red rose is a declaration of love. The object of your affection – be it lover, relative, or friend – will be twice as touched by your fragrant offering if you enclose it in a graceful way. Of course, any single flower can be presented this way. Celebrate the

first day of spring by giving your Significant Other a daffodil. Wrap up an orchid for Grandmom on Mother's Day. Thank a loving friend for a favor done by presenting his or her favorite flower.

How to Make the Rose Package

You'll need a square of glossy white cardboard (see tip on page 59) and the same size square of red paper or tissue. The diagonal measurement of the square should be about one-and-a-half times the length of the rose stem.

Turn the cardboard over, dot with some random drops of glue, and spread the red paper over it.

A. Place the rose on the diagonal, as shown. The broken line here and in the following sketches indicates where your folds should be made. Fold the cardboard and tissue over

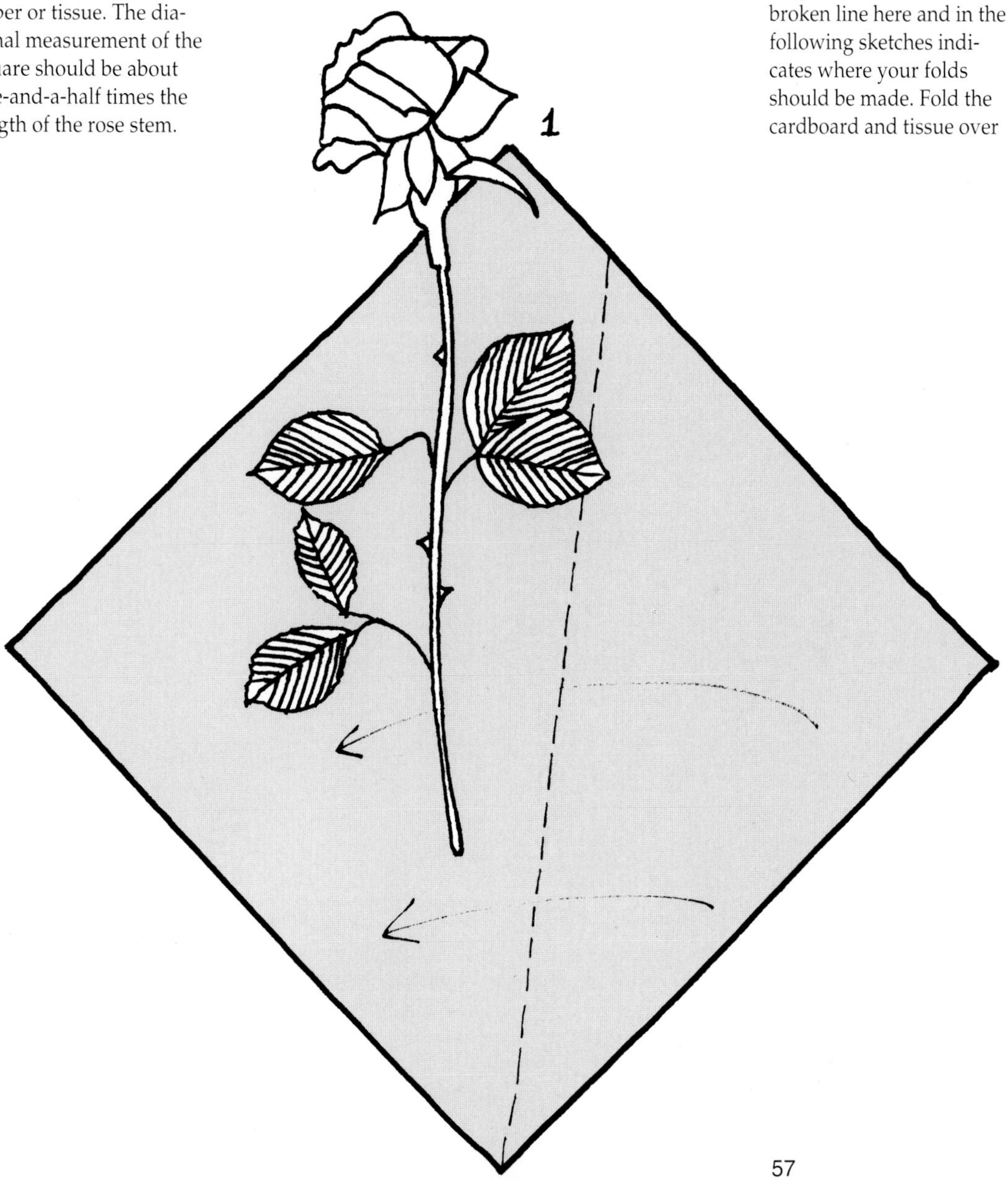

1

2

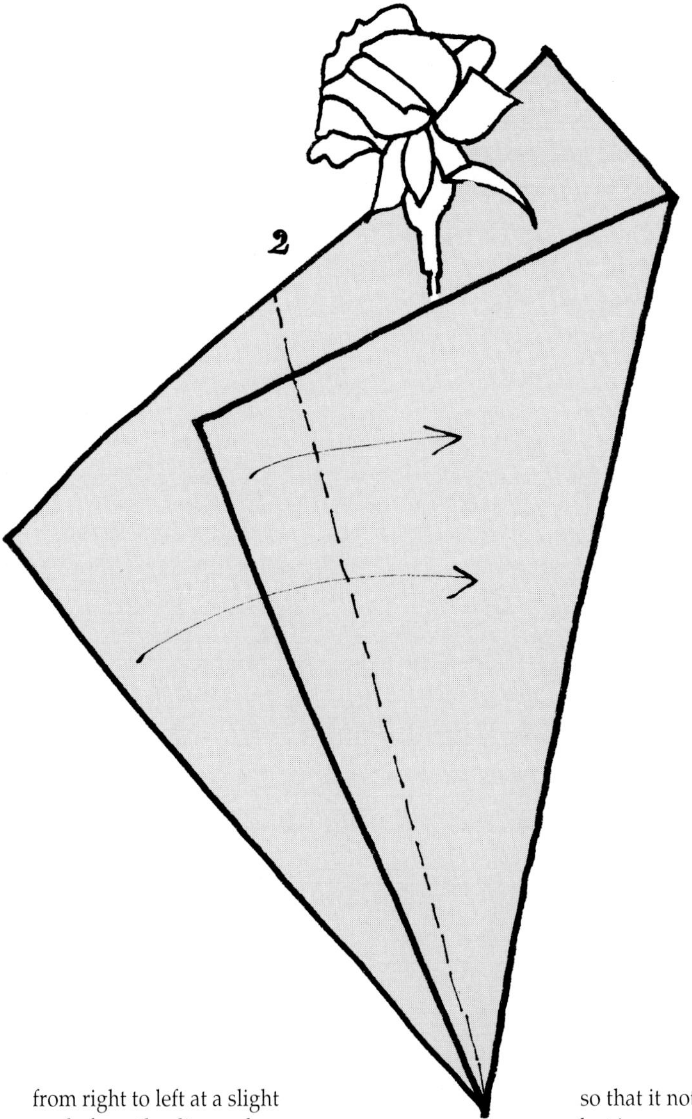

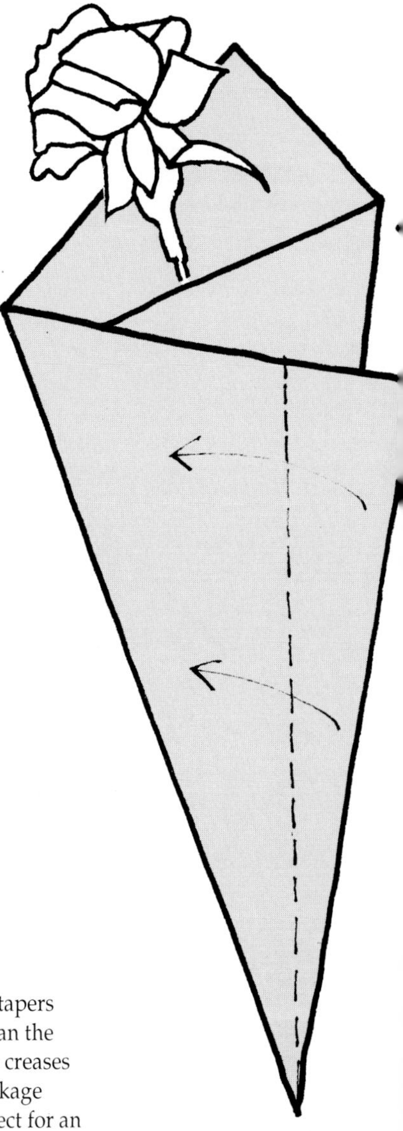

from right to left at a slight
angle from the diagonal.
Crease firmly.
B. Fold left side over right
and crease as shown.
C. Fold back from right to
left and crease as shown.
Notice that the angle of
each fold changes slightly

so that it not only tapers
but is narrower than the
one before. Set the creases
by placing the package
under a heavy object for an
hour or so.
D. Fold the bottom point
under and tape closed.

4

5

1. A very thin cardboard that doesn't need scoring is best for this wrap; look for it at a good art-supply store. Otherwise, a sturdy glossy white wrapping paper will do nicely.
2. If the rose thorns are very sharp, clip them off or they'll tear the liner paper or tissue.
3. Add a spray of fern or baby's breath to your package.
4. Coordinate tissue color to the flower – yellow for daffodil, lavender for orchid, etc.

E. A ribbon decoration finishes this package off beautifully; in this case, a concentric-circle motif made from narrow yellow and silver twine, tied off in a bow and mounted near the bottom of the package. Tuck a rose leaf into one of the folds for final flair.

THE EVENING-PURSE PACKAGE

This elegant box, made from plain cardboard, covered with an Art Deco wallpaper, then trimmed in gold ribbon, is the perfect wrap for a chic oblong gift such as a necklace, silk scarf, silver cake knife, or other flatware serving piece. Remnants or pages from old sampler books can sometimes be obtained from wallpaper dealers. You might have to look around for a while to find what you want, but the effort will be worth it in the unique package that results. Also check out garage and tag sales, and ask friends if they have remainders of vintage wallpaper rolls up in the attic.

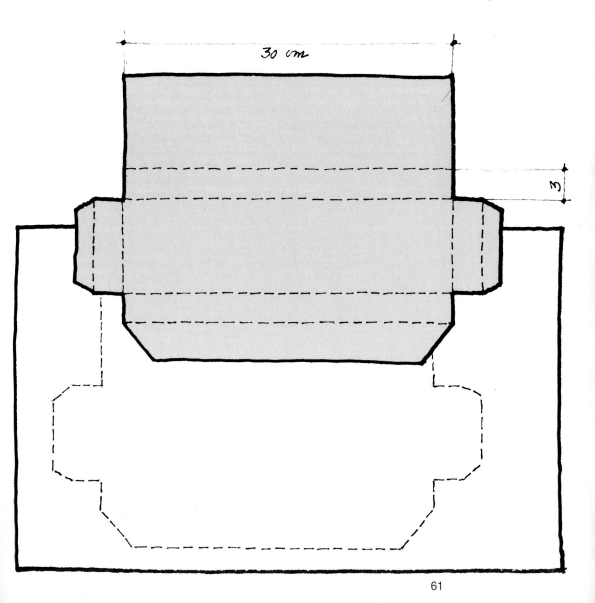

30 cm

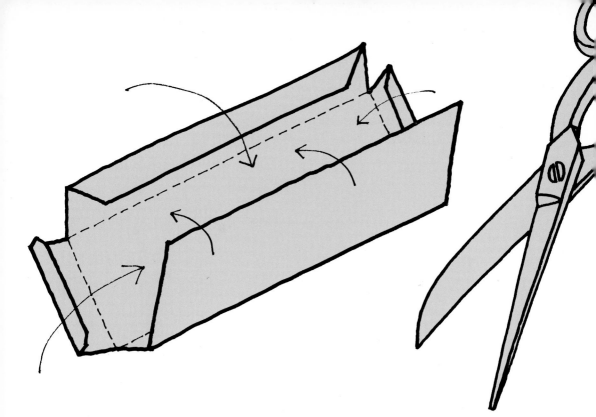

How to Make the Evening-Purse Package

The size cardboard you start with should be calibrated to the gift. Any of the above items would fit into a box base about 12 inches (30 cm) long, the dimension used in the illustration, so start with a cardboard sheet of about 12 by 30 inches (30 by 50 cm). Cut a sheet of wallpaper of the same size. If it's a directional pattern, take into account how it will position on the finished box. Paste the paper to the cardboard and smooth down evenly so that no air bubbles remain.

A. On the reverse side, rule in the basic outline of the box, following the broken-line shape in the illustration.

B. Cut the entire shape out with sharp scissors (a hobby knife might damage the wallpaper on back). Cut off corners as indicated. Take a steel ruler and hold it against each broken line you've drawn for the folds, and score each with the end of a large paper clip.

C. Bend the board inward along your scored lines and crease each fold sharply. Fold in sides and side flaps; fold the front over and glue it to the flaps. Hold these joins in place with big paper clips or clothespins until the glue sets.

D. Decorate the top of the purse: Fold a length of ribbon back and forth in decreasing figure-eight loops and staple it to the box lid. Insert your gift (perhaps wrapped in tissue), close the lid, and place ribbon around the box, covering the stapled loop with a simple bow.

Tips

1. Coordinate ribbon color to the dominant color of your wallpaper pattern. If you want a frilly rather than tailored look, make a big rosette instead of the looped trim.

2. If you can't find Art Deco or other old wallpaper remnants, use a contemporary design. Shops and showrooms that carry wallpaper often have large sam- ple swatches on hand. Friends and family who have recently redecorated are also good poten- tial sources.

3. If you have trouble folding your purse-box together because the cardboard plus wallpaper is too thick, score it carefully on the papered side as well, using a blunt butter knife, an empty ball- point pen, or the end of a large paper clip.

Papers

An endless, ever-changing array of wrapping papers can be found in gift and greeting-card shops, variety, stationery, discount, and department stores, and even some supermarkets. They include solids, metallics, and textured finishes; contemporary and traditional patterns; stripes, plaids, and geometrics; and seasonal designs for just about every holiday on the calendar. Tissue paper and crepe paper come in a rainbow of shades and make appropriate outer wraps as well as useful package stuffing. Wallpaper is also excellent for wrapping. Look for remains of rolls at garage sales; wallpaper showrooms and shops sometimes have ready-to-discard sample books; ask friends who have recently redecorated if they have overage paper to spare. And whenever you have a chance to rummage through someone's attic, you may find rolls of decades-old wallpaper treasures. There are other castoff papers that make imaginative gift wraps, too. Just a few examples are: a road map to enclose a bon-voyage present; tearsheets from the Yellow Pages for a gift of an address/telephone book; the color comics from the Sunday paper for a child's gift.

Cardboard

For constructing your own boxes, art-supply stores offer the best choice of materials. More widely available at variety and stationery stores are cardboards under various names – oaktag, poster board, cover stock, or card stock.

Ribbons

Most variety stores and small card shops stock two basic types of ribbon: satin and ridged curling ribbon in one or two widths. While this book shows how to make bows and rosettes, you can also find an assortment of deluxe ready-made multi-looped bows with self-stick backings. Specialty shops and the notions counter in larger department and chain stores offer a wider variety of ribbon widths, colors, and patterns, as well as other materials for ties, including twine, raffia, colored and metallic cord, and thick yarn. And remember to recycle when you can. Save and reuse lovely bows and ribbons from gifts you receive.

Tapes and Glue

For its functionality, transparent adhesive tape is indispensable to the craft of gift wrapping. Two-sided tape is recommended for a seamless look. It's also useful for tacking big bows and other trim to a package. Colored tapes can be both practical and decorative when combining sheets of different colors or patterns, as is suggested often in these pages. Sometimes glue is preferable, as in giving plain cardboard a silver finish by gluing aluminum foil to it. A white paste, which spreads easily and dries clear, is a good choice. Crafts professionals often use rubber cement, also called paper cement, which is applied with a brush. Papers sealed with it can be peeled apart (for correction) without damage by applying thinner, which must be bought separately – both sold at art-supply stores.

Trim

Dried florals, grasses, leaves, and ferns make pretty-as-a-picture gift trim. Buy them at florists or department stores, or prepare your own by pressing fresh blossoms or leaves in books, or dry them in a warm oven, then use clear spray fixative or metallic spray paint to make them permanent. Leaves dried by nature and collected from the ground are timely for autumn gifts, and what could be a better trim for a winter gift than pine cones, berries, and evergreen sprigs? Tuck silk or other artificial flowers into a puff of tulle or lace to top a spring or summer gift. Other trim to delight gift recipients at any time of year are self-stick decals available in beautiful, cute, old-fashioned, or mod motifs – or make your own by cutting eye-catching visuals from magazines to adorn the next gift you create. Ordinary white self-stick mailing labels are a perfect material from which to make your own decals in basic geometric shapes, then color them with felt-tip markers.

Tools

Sharp scissors, hobby or utility knife, pencil, and steel ruler are basics. The hobby knife can be the kind that has a thin handle with a replaceable, small steel-blade tip – or a mat knife, a large handle with a replaceable single-edged razor blade inserted at one end. For scoring cardboard before folding it, a large paper clip, blunt butter knife, or empty ballpoint pen are good choices. Triangles, T-squares, and other measuring tools are useful for making boxes, but not essential if instructions in this book are followed. Templates with basic geometric shapes are helpful if you want to make your own decals, as described above, and a cuticle scissors is a handy tool for cutting them out. Color them with felt-tip markers.

Summary

When it comes to a gift, the ways to Wrap It Up are limited only by your imagination. Experiment. Be creative. Uniquely, this is a hobby whose beautiful rewards you can share with everyone on your gift list.